Water from Another Source
Barry Schwabsky

Spuyten Duyvil

New York   Paris

© 2023 Barry Schwabsky
ISBN 978-1-959556-07-7
cover image: Hayley Barker, *Incense (Riverwood 4)*, 2021.
Oil on linen, 100 x 82 in (254 x 208.3 cm).
Courtesy of Hayley Barker and SHRINE (NYC).

Author photograph by Xiaofu Wang.

Library of Congress Cataloging-in-Publication Data

Names: Schwabsky, Barry, author.
Title: Water from another source / Barry Schwabsky.
Description: New York ; Paris : Spuyten Duyvil, [2023]
Identifiers: LCCN 2022054103 | ISBN 9781959556077 (paperback)
Classification: LCC PS3569.C5636 W38 2023 | DDC 811/.54--dc23
LC record available at https://lccn.loc.gov/2022054103

For Andrea Applebee, reader/advisor

Contents

II.

III

IV

V

For it would be possible to describe the whole world without mentioning any particular thing.
—Frank Ramsey

CAN A SOUND FRAME ANOTHER SOUND?

The chatter of a thousand crickets frames
the intermittent thrum of one woman's breathing
framed by the chatter of a thousand crickets

I

Is there a face in music?
—*Thelonious Monk*

Two Lips Pronounce One Word

A true poet would destroy the world utterly
crack the silence around
the poem after the last poem
as if lost breath were real being

a falling leaf is what I am
clumsy fingers of the breeze
bury me in sleepless sleep
resplendent under cloud cover

and only now you tell me
my sound makes no sense
what seeing believes is just that

the devil has the best details
he met me back there in the weeds
and called out *cloudhead, cloudhead!*

GOODBYE RHYTHM CHANGES

Music over, papers in order
bitter moments powdered with sugar
chewing abolition in advance
ready to pull scattered bones together

sounds with no rhythm in their step
a bitter light in the middle of the sky
just a drizzled noise, its final texture
a rain you heard tell of

seven come eleven: my double on the road
tried to write me out of the progression and
much said he and I just listened

took very seriously his calm and comradely suggestions
missed the maternal music of your clouded face
the final flower of my sleepless night

ANOTHER SUNSHINE

A banner year for potato bugs
I don't know became our favorite melody
hummed it slowly over and over under my breath
our old gods were hardly strong enough

we offered ourselves threads of aid and comfort
later wrote this in a hurry, postponed drawing
peering into the shadows of a beige hotel room
see first nothing, then everything at once

confused about my own anatomy
fresh memories lifted
from the bottom of a long flight of stairs

the empty place I set at dinner
lost occasion for some more exact silence
and hints of the savor of happy mud

Zero as a Color

I predict the spirit world outlasts us
its silence makes its way slowly, tenderly
little world no one ever owned
the eye, a living shadow

but if we talk of higher adventures
rumors from the place where everything cold happens
as light invests the whispered-to moon
it opens fuller than full

the face on the page is quite blurred
arrives quite naturally when it should
and stays immobile where you last glimpsed it

if we survive the worst
in the eyes of others, that's progress
quietly, the visible part of your childhood melts away

Music for Dilettantes

The end user wore a mask of flamboyant ill-health
as the burden of anticipation began to lift
eyes alone said a prayer for hypochondriacs
and showed their stark naked absence to the world

so much we have in common
a stance of artistic procrastination
meant to prove something in a gesture, for instance
that there's a secret locked behind the mirror

we called desire or music
its notes or chromatic silence meant for your ears only
like vowels heaving with unheard vibrations

decoded on piano and reflected in pale wet eyes
classic blue as Pantone color of the year
a delicate reckoning somewhere 'round about midnight

Life as a Flotation Device

People also ask: what does *obsequious sycophant*
mean? what does *effulgence* mean?
what does *apodictically* mean?
how do you use *apoplectically* in a sentence?

as if a camera could begin to take an interest
in what it sees
that was me until today
I shape an image of you as the entire sky

falls into nothing and wait
with more fear than a minute can hold
for the police to show up

until then my solipsism keeps me busy
molding found sobs into a solo jazz project
the ill-timed tomorrow of another flashing light

CONFESSIONS OF A DEMIURGE

These objects that claim to excavate me
like thoughts that flicker when you look away from them
that come too quickly then go totally white
we call this knowledge by accident

that vain attempt to pick threads of wisdom from live air
back then I was stuck in the coming world
working from home where everything's dirty
and surviving translation into remnants of performance

still happy with sunken colors and drifting shapes
we'll drink this sea-dark wine
but "music paints the frame" (writes William Benton)

the sun's kisses have teeth
between them and their captions of nothing
comes the invented absence of an outside world

Why I Bite My Fingernails at the Movies

Crows fly sideways in the wind
tomorrow takes care of itself, approaching intimacy
wings flap with difficulty toward the present
a place for everything and all out of place

form characters of a most ancient script
or glide on a confluence of codes
where there is nothing, I see something
the spot where even earth sprouts feathers

I know that poetry is better than working
the book drenched in shadow
daylight moon flustered by clouds

waxing gibbous looked similar here
keeping me who I am is not the way my heart so
soft, contiguous, thanks you for not listening

BEES BEWARE!

In lyrics dredged up from an unresolved past
and desultory chat about the even vaguer future
we heard slow sounds of bodies softly touched with paint
prognosis shifting from moderate to severe

they thrive on our abundant sunshine and identical days
ritual worship of ancestors and forgotten gods
their grammar aspirational, at worst a mystic mistake
an insect buzzing in the privacy of your ear

oh nation of bees, your emergency queen consorts with
none but the most rambunctious of passing ghosts
they soak the moving air and its unspoken holdings

but unlike what others call flash bangs
such calm disasters star almost no one
warnings fail in everything but not in metabolizing life

Silence in Mind

Stamped papers still in order
again today forgot to die
my eyes a bit blurrier now
and partly belong to the blurry fields

accepting whispers from all over creation
in casual self-radiance eating
a childish dish of caramel custard
declares all beauty now ancient or post-ongoing

the unfinished reader assigns herself a part in the past
her body an indelible surface exposed
to common air that hides this truth from you

maximum dawn exerts some pressure toward futures
lingering fastidiously on the wire
you can see them anywhere out of this window

Me/Anti-Me

This skin is not, has never been my own
it found me naked on the ground
the heart's chamber a cenotaph
the demonic rhythm of its beating a plausible fiction

muffled clatter of ping pong balls
I keep wondering if I'm meant to pursue
the past ambles by in kitten heels
leans over to wipe the mirror clean

I have no intention of trying to sample
our meantime for future reference
optical cloth caressing reflected human skin

brushed east one day, west another
my certificate in the dreaming arts
meantime the scale of sunlight: monumental

DOWN WITH ORIGAMI!

Forced by the circumvention of time
bethought more angels than you could ever handle
then boom!—a glimmer of voices under heavenly rain
advice unbought for love or money

m'lord dug up the bones of your ancient glory
in this sheet the crease resembles a mountain
later melts into a warbling landscape
this life is not the safest hideout

you're always slipping out of its flaps and folds
but not to have the last word
I insist on my despair, bitch

in fact I don't deserve the added overtones
curled between the margins of a book I stole as a teenager
and shelved at random in the house of migraine

Season Two, Episode Six

Naiads lie, the alien said
a wordless voice from beyond the bedroom
and with death at ease in our midcentury modern
the future continues to burn

those days when rain never stopped blowing sideways
the book flew into your room
the happiness there was deafening
it told us everyone's still invited

but not all will come right away or ever
in those simpler days we did what we could
fixed the moon inside a frame

some quiet located 0.2 miles down on your left
cushioned against the dangers of a dream and locked away
an oracle pronounced slowly backward word by word

Synopsis of the Last Poem

The world stays wicked
not a promise but a threat
the thought of your thought
a story getting longer, action over or not

a shadow flickering on the ceiling
stays stuck in its unhappy boyhood of words
sex is a dragonfly hovering
things move, shadows so long in progress

just do what everyone else does
but stop to feed the companion
your well-seasoned memories

some people will always be children
their bodies not made for the superfluous
the unknown world that disappears with you

II

Countries on the brink of destruction and peoples given up for lost are not without music, but their music is not music.
— The Springs and Autumns of Master Lü
(*translation by Haun Saussy*)

II

Voir Dire

Explain how the statue came down
later carried dripping to an undisclosed location
you can take pictures of all kinds of things
but the utterly beheld

or unbeheld
a life too fast to keep up with
disorienting like the blast of sunlight
when you exit the darkness of a movie theater in the afternoon

you ask how we survive all this surviving
with unlimited desire for freedom
and a name that might have been onomatopoeia
an official divulged that there are no planned fixes

snails and butterflies begin to emerge
from a single-use epic written
backward in the fog on a mirror
the all and more-than-all

sounded out with hesitation from the other side
an echo of someone's laughter in the beat of your heart
if love has but a single face
your noticing is what makes it so

Refugee from a Time Unrecorded

Born at an unknown hour
childhood in a city whose streets have no names
where current events are rumors transmitted at odd hours on unreliable
        frequencies
and each family speaks its own peculiar dialect
mutually untranslatable

subject once took inspiration from an anonymous book found in the back
        seat of an unlicensed taxi and left in the back seat of another still
        unread
abandoned joy when someone let all the joy leak out of it
later credited with the free invention of a sky park where cirrus clouds
stood vigil all night over lost hours of dreamless sleep when moonlight knit
        each thing together with its shadow

not unlike one of those defeated warlords behind the wheel of an airport taxi
        who intimate only to randomly selected passengers something of a
        storied past unfortunately stained with more than a bit of blood
a musician wondering what to do after the old tunes have been played and the
        major and minor and diminished chords have been heard but the song
        isn't over, just inaudible
and with the end of any productive conversation with the farthest-flung stars
        a mind drifts in careless eddies beyond thought
to shelter in the impartial shade of a tree on which a phoenix will one day
        land
and having learned something about fear, something about desire, nothing
        about who you might have been otherwise
bid love and hate a well-earned but desperate farewell.

THAT THE DURATION OF LOVE MAY BE GREATER THAN OR EQUAL TO THE LENGTH OF A LIFE

Filled with silt carried downstream
to deposit somewhere
in the shape of a woman
known by face and by name, a womanly woman
and even by the stroke of a brush or an eyelash
you always wished could paint you into existence
or gather you into its cunning shadow

this picture is truly a lamentation
not unlike the face of farewell
in which at the last moment you hope to recognize
a happy end awaiting you
in bloodstains arranged tone by tone
on the palette of aromas of flesh
you remember endlessly in air-conditioned quarantine
in your lucky palace of storms

a nearly noiseless encounter
as in memory you kissed one and forgot the rest
watched a future drown in a river of blue ink
a future close as tongue to lip
as lip to nipple
as nipple to tooth
under closed eyes
and a crown made of butterflies

From a Fourth-Floor Walk-Up

In this sumptuous parody of distressed creation
birds croaking like the ghosts I can't stop fighting
beneath an impatient veil of sky
as ruined as it is celebrated
trade clashing diagnoses

you taste just like that
the tints and shades of merciless silence
essential oils of citrus and clove
a delicate brocade of confusing color

your face, heraldic with praise and scorn
voice with a river view
vexed by shadows of an enormous thirst
almost always the shape of your name

as it slowly wraps itself in the warm folds of a forgotten time
hungry for commotion that never seems to begin
but it's happening
in the sleeplessness of the trees
a patience with the darkness deepening under branches

Revocation of the Previous Privacy Policy

A slashing light left its vanishing mark
in a poem secretly forged in your name
where even loneliness finds its perfection
products and services we think you might like

a solar body gathers dust in the reading
its scandal or wonderment
the way water looks you in the eye
trembling
in the high tide of a fallacy

or paints the passing portrait of a thought
still unfinished
and who cares if it's clothed or naked
consolation or reprisal
and whose soul enters whose body

a kind of gray religious feeling
against a planar scarlet surface
dishes clinking, phones ringing
we listen with a common ear

what else could we do but veer off
into what's true outside on the street
where the facts already known
have been released into the wilds of time
so we will not withhold judgement
long since lodged

eleven thousand lightning strikes
lit what never looked like tinder

The Open Sweater Chronicles

Truth with its most annoying habits
humor bleeds into cruelty
like a double exposure
moon rising over the escarpment

noisy scenes of a silent city
its providential spaces
or forced heaven
your nostalgia for the sun

but seeping in from our forgotten future
the sun just turns its back
old moments left out to dry
shadows hang over the eyelids

you sing into pale blue skies
of places dark and cold
trees losing all sense of time
they complain of the excessive heat

An Author's Love Note to Her Typesetter

Please don't forget you're just my poetry beast
the ambivalent nude who always disdains the inessential
no shame to compose a tenebrous wonder on movable type
tracing love's plenitude back to its most distant sources
nor blame the trees for the pages we made from them

but enough of your damned simplicity
I heard not knowing is your favorite thing to do
please find the enclosed poems that lock you out, keep you
in the open where I can observe you
pouring solar liquid in the ear of a ragged day

it's an inappropriate tear that grieves for unmade plans
actually just the call of a distant bird
that warbling's not our music
it says the sky wants to fuck the earth
but your body walks my mind in the direction of death

don't hope to find me there
another cosmos under the roof of my mouth
just because we love flowers doesn't mean
lay them on the grave of bitter thoughts
I know as the rounded surface of your eye

The Future Will Not Forgive Us

Why the Golden Gate Bridge made strange noises—put that
in your open book of witty sayings
I thought she'd pour a little drop of poison on my tongue
a stone mirror shows the cruelty in a forlorn smile's untruth
they dreamed they were autochthonous, souls heaved
up from the soil into darkness
their ciphers and protocols implicate other people, not you
whose failure to uphold your own obsolescent values
may be your most charming attribute

nothing to say about that, nothing much to know
strange as it seems, my other brain is a pinwheel galaxy
a deep-sky stellar factory most faint
on the edge of the perceivable
it's elsewhere everywhere
and the only mystery
how did it come to this

this hummingbird lodged deep in my throat
hummingbird lodged itchily in my scrotum
hummingbird lodged fluttering in my asshole
gave me the courage to say that
to wonder how many ounces of meaning
you baked in with each word
recapturing the childhood aroma that automatically brings comfort
which he won't name in case you later use it to fool him

THE SORE-THROATED SINGER TO HER LOVERS

Drawn out from transparent conversation
and but poorly armed with tears

a sound that's the opposite of thunder
fine dust falls on the beauty of outside

a cloudy lake gathers time in its lap
mist is but faint praise for a forest

your soul pressed between two futures

listen won't work, later be no singing
breeze lets saplings brush the sky

like the echo of your footsteps
this silence lurks behind your back

the clock strikes midnight once an hour

EVERYTHING BUT

Will they go back to writing about flowers and moons?
—Viet Thanh Nguyen

Decline and fall revisited, a time beyond recognition
they've already begun remembering me
in the odors of a burnt-out forest where
you administer creative deficiencies

ideas that touch only where they're broken
keep talking to myself but don't listen
sipping tea cooled with blood and cream
they start eye-gazing

and (paused, ghostly image) never stop
the preceding verse should be reduced in level
filtered slightly darker to make the transition clearer
fire runs away up the hill singing

how far America lies from my heart
I spy the sublime of miniaturization in the pupil of an eye
where stormy skies welcome balmy weather
and hard work only makes it worse

an eye is a moon in all its phases
and that tiniest reflection in it
is it just me? or the roses I proffered
with love, an unnatural business

reassuring myself against the landscape
a music built just of chords that assail the world
in my final days of healing
use a rose as my microphone

Ritual of Disappearance

Addressing every word by name
this calm terrestrial face, firm but fair
accepts even what you think you can't

the outstretched hand, a thought as big as air
the book pulled down from the highest shelf
two-body motion being always planar

communicable colors break loose
through a tiny crack in the plaster wall
stray notes of a bright but desiccated music

dark pockets you keep turning inside out
for the unhappy ending where things
start to look more similar to themselves

you are not there to be written to
whose heart is yet an unripe fruit
yes, agreed, there's something incredibly funny

about being, just being
they say you're nowhere until
you're everywhere and that's only

when evening stirs lazily on the horizon
pretty voice and not much to do with it
teasing a flame that shivers constantly

a click track for your ears only
birds hang at loose ends declaring their exuberance
rising vapors adorn the residence of time

and gather as a fog installed between us
feeling that something very chancy had arrived
and you stopped to ask what was it

THE GATHERING OF THE POEM

Anonymous winds shake the house
I nod and hand you this furtive book
swallowed phrases stretched tight like a membrane
caught the damp light that lit my dream each night

in which I always forget to reply
meanwhile see how death claims
your old abandoned work as his own
signs my name to it twice, top and bottom

for him these are quiet times
vexing news unheard but for
the slim satisfaction of making enemies
phatic or fatal as you choose

times gazing out at muffled memories in the distance
why the moonlit sky looks so unhappy
deceptive apparition of a present
our pooled chaos needs a deep spring cleaning

WINE WITH EVERYTHING

To earth's favorite enemy
time's phosphorescent bride
happiness is a warning against
drowning in the silence of a more pensive face

this attenuated mind
long delayed in its privacy
now pours out from everywhere
an imitation in moisture of the gathered economic flux

lipstick-warmed voice, its hinged expressions
lost in amorous nightfall
hating everything I agree with
my language seen through a dirty window

but you can't drown in the same river twice
let fury have its way for a moment
the all having been reduced to many
the best spot to see it from is here

FLIES IN THE FACE

The sole beginning, this one:
a face lit by two drifting planets
death hardly noticed my disappearance
these scraps of a painted landscape

a little tune I call pure consciousness
its melody behind a veil
a momentary intonation
just to ask the simplest thing

there's a blush on the horizon
some roses offered to the muse of laziness
crows held at a fabricated distance

drawing profit from a passing cloud
is this something or nothing or in between
the shrimp must be deveined

DID I SEND YOU THIS?

So the landscape seems curtained
sits back to admire itself mirrored
in an afternoon of smoke and water
waits to see where the vapors drift off to
or condense into my bone marrow

the counterworld where lost or unattended thoughts reside
in low light thoughts float in invisible bubbles above the heads
of pensive words that calmly go about their business
I keep looking or listening for your unsigned preface to my intentions

kind of chilly in this room there's no more room in
cool or warm as a neon mouth
love's whispers keep me awake at night
and morning comes too early again

WATER FROM ANOTHER SOURCE

If only I had never vanished
what wouldn't you remember
the adoration extracted
from a dance of the one and the two

infused into these veins
music begins only in darkness
as a scent in the air
oil of phosphorus on the hands

grace and favor in the narrow eyes of a cat
we could play divinity or demiurge
the initiative is yours
no light can cut us off

from our old banished shadows
the kind heart is intransitive
a more perfect din than ever
your mind a smile that warns me
you are the water and the thirst

III
In Memory
of the Last Poem

On cold but chilly mornings, vermillion in the shadows.
—*Pierre Bonnard*

In one unreliable account
what passes for poetry

precision strikes
up to a point

images pay no rent
but the echo carries

from what distance
could a cloud of dust
look that hard—

"His own people"
the flower is you
"in this enormous hospital"
yet again
(as I said before)
truth can be recombined
inside a shadow
plush without testament
your line drawings of air
help bear the heat of love—

Once before running out of breath
matching sky against sky

"if your mind is not paranoid these days"
you've got a big problem

scantily represented in the literature
of bridge and tunnel lyricism

not particularly frightened by my death
—the rest I think you know

in an atlas of cold weather
drawn to its inconclusion

powdered eye
don't ask me about it now—

Your footsteps take me a long way
on the radio I hear money singing
wish I had more too
an art for people who don't know anything about it
if only you were in front of me
I wouldn't be able to look into your eyes
I was hoping for glorious gleeful failure—

~~The moon is real~~
~~the moonlit ghost is real~~
~~but like a soft lens~~
in place of the words you lost
it was never me
the one you heard talking

who knows who likes their sex with who—

Winter torn to bits
flickers down as propaganda
unrecovered thoughts
gathered in heaps around cars and bushes
but who cares
even most whitened colors
grow leaden in the shadows—

Hello forever
goodbye for now
whose name was never known
overhead for personal items
there's no place like noplace
someone call the pleasure police because
mine's been stolen—

Let's do it wrong again
one last time
and turn out the light
but pay no mind
recite
our last poems
outlast poems—

IV

La musica non è un'arca sulla quale ci si possa salvare del diluvio.
—*Walter Marchetti*

VI

Six Poems with a Line from Sappho

I. Not Yet Human

But one must risk everything, since
the eye loses the plain sense
at the end of a sentence previously unknown
or a word that keeps its eye on me
though not yet quite human

preparing for the great leap out of your body
you spend your longest days
trapped inside a shorter one, dodging thoughts
buried in the previous day's graveyard
it happens all the time in fiction
I could tell you'd been there

where in time you wait to be consumed
hear the chattering migration of so many birds
excited with the sound of the ocean
love is a strange language when you speak it
with such a flat and neutral accent

say what?—whether to be the last
of the first or first of the last
she was brutally dressed
singing things to be afraid of
door cracked or wide open, what difference
we'll be our own guests

II. You Remind Me of Me

Shy voice behind sunglasses
your dark smile reminds me of me
saying one must risk everything, since

light takes the fast lane
eye threatened by handmade colors
the future cannot describe

wipe the dust off my voice
and shine it up nice
close sky feels almost like rain

blunt waves finger the sand
eyes only mirror the moment
a liar and who can blame me

III. Take Pleasure in Waiting

Night wakes up bleary-eyed
looks at where you used be
stretched diagonally across the unmade bed
your well-padded labyrinth

where one must risk everything, since
a Minotaur you're still in love with
lurks outside in search of a door
knowing hope is only for the hopeless

a body unearthed from
the humified substance of sleep
dark, spongy, and jelly-like
without determinate shape, structure, or quality

the sentence holds no dominion
the ear has a back door to the throat
clouds dusted with charcoal
slumber lightly on the horizon

IV. We Abolish the World of Appearances

Heard across an iridescent boundary
trees from which the crows issue their warning
something stirring in the garden
sometimes the sky moves

one night under tumbling wind
found me carefully folded up in your pocket
which is not a breathable world

police sirens sound like ghosts
accumulating as spacious dreams in which
a hesitant soul can roam at large
a drastic mind wanders

you would have spilled the rhythm
but one must risk everything, since
if tomorrow remembers the truth

there will be poetry like it or not
the omega of the inner eye
dawn, flagrant in the trees
pokes the red sun right in the eye

V. FLOCCINAUCINIHILIPILIFICATION

This time last year
a veiled rumbling
none of this will ever be remembered
except in thoughts so small and unwise

clouds in this dream are something other than grey
she said the sea has no form
dark music in which all tones are possible
and none sounded

no, death is not the saddest story of all
but fear, the best stone to build with
and where can I get some more
at least asleep we might be innocent

one must risk everything, since
we know how it is to accumulate
that acrid smell of burnt ideas
weather's getting so dangerous

VI. TWEE REVISITED

Last day in an empty room
existence has yet to be surpassed
while waiting for more storage to be added
new worlds, new life
it all happens so fast
the quick minute between cocktails and dinner

so we sink into the plush chords of a folkie serenade
sound veiled in static
like a soft hairy mass you roll yourself up in
the past is here
solidified as a breathing body
its words had never crept into any poem before

head made of snow
we wait for that sweet trivial feeling coming back
mopey, unpredictable
recall your original aspiration
a friendlier star would shine a light
much softer than a rainy morning

but one must risk everything, since
nature's just a silly song
we always used to sing
a heavenly word we mispronounced

HAPPY SNOW DAY

The ones who saw and entered the building
words we said and came to regret
you'd expected a knock at the door
or the bell of someone's name to ring

alarmed to see yourself asleep
a character hard to reconcile
with waiting out the day in hiding
mistreatment attends a swoony melody

out there the great unknown is back in style
sky the color of your former eyes
clouds you seemed to shape by hand
industrial noises deep in the background

scattered exclamations overheard
us through a cracked window
music out of nowhere settles among
pots and pans, snap and stop

building is an abyss you take for granted
this nightmare's name is not the world
persuasive shadow love pursuit by omission
totally friends fake fur mirror play

PAGES FROM A JAPANESE PHOTOBOOK

Ever-waning presence
an exasperated taste for simplicity
its oily yet grainy mouthfeel
like when your dull voice
plumbs my throat, deep

no future in the mirror
without shoes these ghosts
most welcome in the silence
each too immature for the other
their poses Elizabethan, melancholy

can't bear to stop them
or trouble their difference with
smiled assumptions of respect
relieved salutations of
the possible, ignored

a horizon left in shreds
when beauty exceeds imagination
its touchpoint holds stubborn
a nail your sweater's caught on
you need a face trained in happiness
to manage that, almost

FOR THOSE WHO ARE STILL ALIVE

Learn to give up living on cigarettes alone
unwrap the human flesh from around a hopeful
machine vision
your future draws you irresistibly
toward the conclusive fund of memories
in a drier city you'd have to know how to breathe
stone, drink dust
a thirst for unpeopled alleyways
in everything you do

How to Let Go of Time

Look deep
into the sun-drenched eye
no staring now
what color is your iris
the color of everything
only the blue aches with memory
a sphincter muscle to constrict or dilate the pupil
an ache in which truth reveals
a word to be translated
by whoever
feels a fog stuck in their throat

look deep
into the eye of the future
the one place
midnight lasts forever
your darlings all immortal
grace and favor won't watch the clock
a true storm
felt the ache of time
flooding down from the sky
things I'd never want to control
I said you were my freedom
to paint with the color of everything
memories that will hereafter be censored

sunken reflections
another fluorescent moment
yet so much like you
in the week since I left my body
I lost all interest in work

building clouds out of spare colors
the eye desires
a place in the mud
the mud had forgotten
it's not true you can make nothing of it
though it can be safely assumed
a thing can only be made of things

rendezvous with a goblin child
whose body changes color every day
and can't hold still for hunger
or fear of the violence of men
who said it would go hard with me
that madness is the need to be desired
the minute you wake up
or the hope of keeping form alive
in a museum housed in a dream
of the lunatic freedom of time

REST ON THE FLIGHT INTO EGYPT

for Monica Ferrando

What if I were to film you all the time
even waking up the hard way
from a dream into another wandering dream
no north, no south, an empty data set
from which ancient aromas exhale
the terrain seemed unbounded
no such sky, no such sun

and if afterward you forgot how to
keep believing what you saw
and never expected anyone else to hear
the note as clear as a diamond in a cloud
and alive to the high-pitched vibration
that set even shadows atremble
remembered despair lit you up from within

From the Downtown Flower District

All the clocks are running down
buds still blossom in silence
let me feel your touch while my body's still
near perfect

set knowledge in the past tense
keep it warm and porous, dear heart
and call it a night

they want to thank us for this emotion
at least we'll die simultaneously
followed by a temporary resurrection
warm and porous

love was an aroma that filled the room
or a natural shelter, maybe a juniper tree
furnished with lava lamp

meant to ask for the most private bouquet
all the tenses switched off at once
ringing in my ears made me forget whatever it is
I used to know

there is no world but the world
a quantum space, frothy and quietly churning
in the ever-changing eye of another planet
inaudible turquoise, azure, robin's egg, celestial
like oxytocin

Soundtrack for a Seascape

Breathing was never that easy
it's said you once lived in water
according to a breathless calendar
timeless corridors of waves upon waves

life on earth comes to its glorious end
wondering why a certain sound is dealt a certain name
homophony of longing for the moon
the left hand's exasperated resistance to the wind

the sun caught napping, an ocean disassembled
its freezing point decreases as salt concentration increases
the best notes are always unnecessary
salt enters through the pores

a sudden thirst for quotations
some regrets I never managed to feel
flood tide makes its way toward the sky
drapes in warm fluid a planet you won't know how to miss

V

WATER SPILLED FROM SOURCE TO USE
—Lawrence Weiner

THE POEM IN THE MIRROR

Such heavy shadows
their weight bends the branches
my skin in shreds
drips slowly to earth
waits for words to arrive
the hours we didn't spend talking

this fat world has eyes for you
at first I thought those stars were teeth
it's true by now that everything's gone retro
your theory provides for each possible outcome
earth slowly sheds its skin
your spirit starts to show the cold air its bones

LOST IN A PAINTING

for Hannah Beerman

In a painting made of things
the thing with most plasticity
is still paint. But the space
a painting makes out of things
is less than the space things imply
in becoming something like
paint. I'm writing your poem,
Hannah, I hope that's alright.
Words are things until

they become paint, until
the interaction of their colors
becomes a fable: two hats affixed
to a stretcher cover the crowns
of heads that must live inside
the wall—a life at right angles
to the one we know. Or what's
bread for hungry eyes is what-
ever you want, whatever you see

flat. What feeds the famished
eye is a puzzled smile or was it
a quick melancholy laugh at
all or some of the beautiful junk
of our climate, now irrevocably
changed, but still a poem in
the frame of its questioning
(which questioning is the poem
itself, if you paint it that way).

My Own Private Grey

Life's honored guest / with no space for thirsty birds / dust as a substance
engulfing shadows / aim your poisoned art / a million years of cruelty
on earth / the real moon identical to the imaginary moon / fantastic
little invention / your memory of the water sisters / self-illuminated
or self-darkened as the case may be / all these roaring years / time
passes with flying colors: blue, cinnabar, orange / your body is the most
pressing argument for / what in me belongs to anyone else / an alphabet
not for us to learn / time burnt out on sound / between before and after

RIDDLE

for Raúl Cordero

It's in my possession
but it's not my possession
it's yours for free
worthless or priceless?
try it on your tongue
salty or sweet?
if swallowed
it might lodge near the heart

THE MIRROR IS YOUR FAVORITE POEM

The spirit freezes up in your bones
the floor was dried-out skin
your faith shows what can be done
now everything's gone, it's true
at first I thought the stars had teeth
your fate should have paid you closer attention

we didn't talk for long
or wait for further word to come
the earth was slowly retreating
my skin began to crack
its weight gives strength to the branches
your shadow feels so heavy

Queen of Swords Reversed

The red-maddened sky at morning / mistaking one god
for another / an enunciation beyond compare / every picture
kills a story / link in my bio / it happens all the time
in fiction / your stuttering apocalypse / if you're anything
like me anyway / condemned to linger at the shore / to translate
your womanhood into what / hot and cold cunning / or how to kiss
my infection /past present futile / and contend with the shrill voice
of compassion / cow-eyed / choosing harm reduction / asleep
at the horizon line / with actual persons living or dead

Like a Haiku

for Raúl Cordero

Calm
silence
rolls

deftly
through
so much
clamor

roar
echo un-
heard

DIALOGUES, NOTES, AND PARABLES OF A PRODIGAL BEHOLDER

for Sónia Almeida and toward Magnus Frederik Clausen

"I've built a house whose roof has tiny holes in it, each revealing a single star in the night sky. Just think! A house whose ceiling is the celestial darkness ablaze!"

"But don't you get wet when it rains?"

"No, on rainy nights there are no stars to be seen, so there are also no holes."

*

She sat with her back to him, writing a love letter. He couldn't see what she wrote. The sounds of the pen scratching along the paper were the message he heard. Once he'd heard the message she'd written, she burned the letter.

*

"The colors you paint with brighten the room!"

"Really? But the ink you write with darkens thought."

*

"He said, 'I've finally made a painting I can stand behind.' Yes, really. Literally. It wants no wall. He holds it upright while standing behind it, and the best part is, wherever you stand to look at it, he can hold it in front of you. You never see the artist, but he's always there behind it."

"Yes, but behind the artist, there's something unseen holding him up too."

*

Painter to poet: "I've memorized your poem. I know it by heart."

Poet to painter: "Thank you! I remember your painting. It's on the tip of my tongue."

*

The painting of the painting doesn't stop when the painter stops painting: perpetual motion.

*

"Are all questions trick questions?"

"Who's asking?"

*

Like walking around with a sharp, tiny pebble in your shoe—just so, there are irritating little thoughts that get under the sole of your brain.

*

"With this one little word 'is' I can make all the metaphors in the world. But painting lacks the word 'is.'"

"No. It's there but tacitly. It is understood."

"Not by me."

"In language, that 'is' of yours is an instrumentality for making metaphors, but it doesn't function metaphorically itself. Painting shows what 'is' should be a metaphor for."

*

The immobility of an artwork outruns time. Its volatility in perception unsettles space.

*

"Isn't the critic rather like a dentist? Always full of words, words, incessant words, as he pokes his instruments around, his probes and little mirrors, his curettes, as if he really expected you to be able to respond, which his attentions make impossible!"
"... ..."

*

Some poems follow you along as you go, like the moon. Paintings tend to stay in place; they wait for you to come back to them—the prodigal beholder.

*

"What, they want to participate in the work of art? As if the work would not exist without their little action or gesture?"
"No—as if they would not exist without this donation of self."

*

Once, people used to say, "In the next life…" Apparently, this is it.

MEDITATIONS OF A MASK

for Brenda Zlamany

I

At first I thought those stars were teeth
an illegible expression provides for each possible outcome
as earth slowly sheds its skin
in preparation for an interview with the moon
your spirit starts to show the cold air its bones
this fat world has eyes for you

II

Such heavy shadows
their weight bends the branches
my skin in shreds
drips slowly to earth
waits for words to arrive
the hours we spent not talking

III

Drifting late among faceless houses
humid in the bitter simmering of the dispossessed
whose words are a hundred thousand pictures of the coming rain
we'd thought to find their wicked footsteps more abundant
propose a hieroglyphic poetry of bliss
in closer dialogue with their fine and dusty anger

IV

Sky azure blue, a burning color
reaches out to take you by the hand, compassionate
you wonder how the world persists without these memories
where blood leaks from the open moment
so many lovely words I won't know how to pronounce
we hear sounds differently shaded

V

Beneath my aching feet the soil remains firm
shy and lonely death gods take no responsibility
for men whose thoughts are thunder and lightning
indifferent to healing in the pure sine tone known as meanwhile
the one small stretch of time
entirely composed of thought

VI

At least if intel pans out
each residual object would be a listening ear
your eye whispers to
that other dream we requested
the music that will once have taken place
the hours spent swirling in its liberties

VII

Nothing bizarre among the secrets exchanged
no news from the single sparrow
wheeling crazily in the breeze above us
that one thing someone hesitated to say
the movie usually ends by nightfall
the irresponsible hour when darkness shows its flaw

VIII

Call off your noisy angels, please
your pets and stray amniotic beings
the pale horizon, its elusive depths
you gradually press up toward the clouds
the trees we engage in whispering converse
using off-pitch syllables for lack of better

IX

In our rose dream theater official video
the hour need not match its description
your hidden features mark a deeper understanding
eyes as soft as piles of ashes
the threadlike seepage of a telling silence
you can always say no to time another time

HALF PAST PARADISE

for John Newsom

Our roadless travels
where green looked
so much greener
blue more transparent

like a stream
of lost or troubled thoughts
footsteps led to woods
so deep they scared me

the world looked differently
when finally painted
all around me
was only foreground

I turned back
found myself lost notwithstanding
in a flurry of highlights
where ghostly songs wait humming

I deny their existence
but remember
everything that wasn't
already isn't

Acknowledgements

Some of these poems, which were written in 2020 and 2021, have appeared in the following print and online periodicals, on occasion under different titles: *Caesura, Columba, The Fortnightly Review, New Observations, NOON: Journal of the Short Poem, Salt, Tourniquet Review*, and *Volt*; on the website/electronic exhibition *Poems from Instructions*, edited by Guy Bennett; and in the publications accompanying the exhibitions "Standard Error (SE)," by Sónia Almeida and Magnus Frederik Clausen, Tørreloft/AGA Works, Copenhagen, 2020; "The City 'La Ville,'" curated by Madame Anonyme aka Brigitte Nicole Grice, Chez Anonyme, Los Angeles, 2021; and "John Newsom: Nature's Course," Oklahoma Contemporary, Oklahoma City, 2022. "Like a Haiku" was written for Raúl Cordero's installation *THE POEM*, which was installed in Times Square, New York, April 8-May 4, 2022. Special thanks to Times Square Arts and the Times Square Alliance. "Six Poems with a Line from Sappho" and "In Memory of the Last Poem" were published as the chapbook *Two Sequences* by The Song Cave, 2022.

BARRY SCHWABSKY has published four previous books of poetry as well as several chapbooks. He is the author of numerous works of criticism, and is the art critic for *The Nation* and co-editor of international reviews for *Artforum*.

www.ingramcontent.com/pod-product-compliance
Lightning Source LLC
Chambersburg PA
CBHW010220140626
46545CB00014B/3137